THIS BOOK
BELONGS TO

_____

ZION SIGN

1= Dark Brown

2= White

3= Light Brown

ZION

NATIONAL PARK

Zion canyon is over 2,000 feet deep!

WESTERN COLUMBINE FLOWER

1= Red

2= Yellow

3= Green

Columbine comes from the Latin word for "dove". It was named this because the inverted flowers look like five doves clustered together.

ANNA'S HUMMINGBIRD

These hummingbirds can catch up to 2,000 insects a day!

THE NARROWS

1= Blue	3= Green
2= Brown	4= Orange

The Narrows is the most popular hike in Zion

CONDOR

1= Light Brown	3= Dark Brown
2= Yellow	4= Gray

Condors can have a wingspan of up to 10 feet!

SEASONAL CHANGES OF THE GAMBLE OAK LEAVES

1= Green	3= Orange
2= Yellow	4= Brown

Native Americans have used Gambel Oak acorns for ceremonial, food and medicinal purpoases for many years.

HANGING GARDENS

1 = Light Brown	3 = Dark Brown
2 = Light Green	4 = Dark Green

Zion's hanging gardens contain plants with the special ability to grow in rock.

RINGTAIL

1= White	3= Dark Brown
2= Black	4= Light Brown

Ringtails are excellent climbers, capable of ascending
vertical walls, trees, rocky cliffs and even cacti!

ARIZONA SISTER BUTTERFLY

1= White	3= Grey	
2= Orange	4= White	5=White

These butterflies love the oak trees of Zion Canyon

MEXICAN TRE-FOILD FLOWER

1= Red	3= Green
2= Yellow	4= Orange

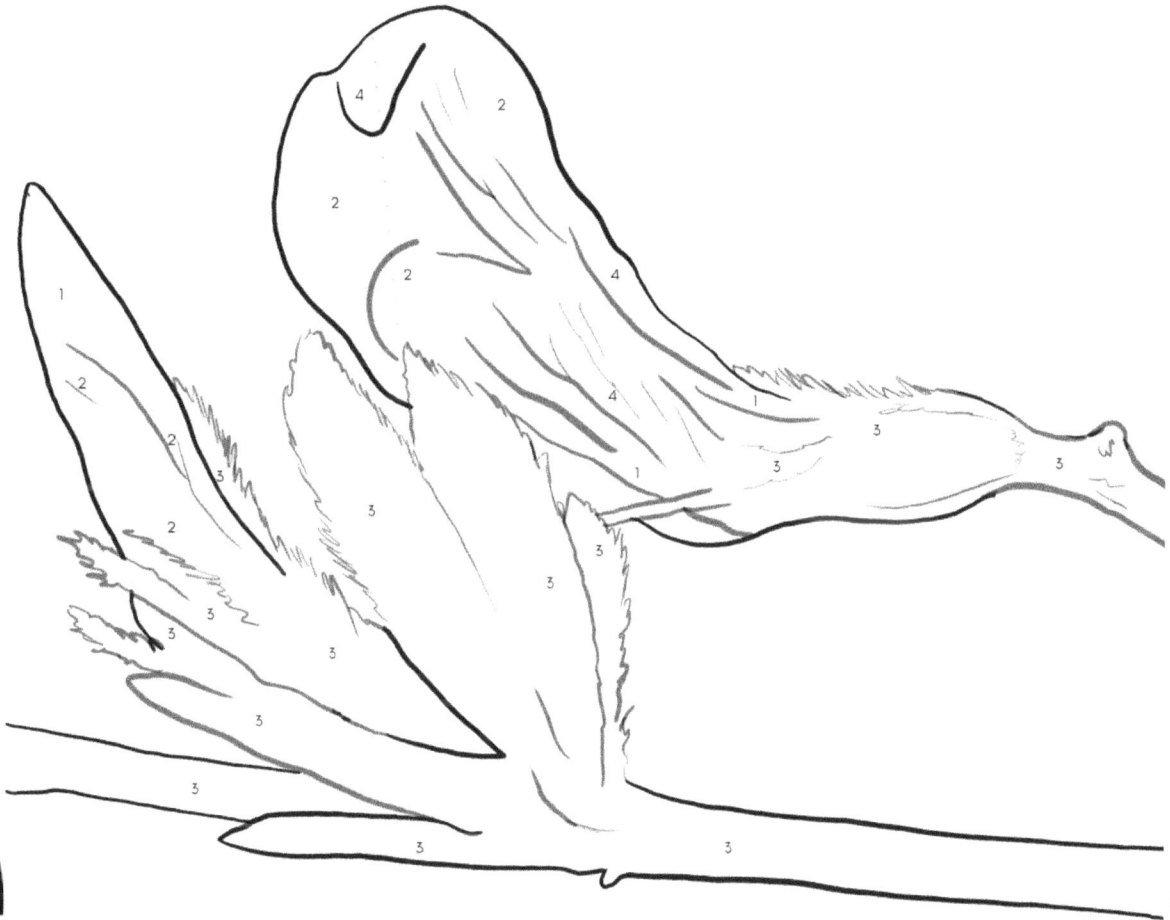

You can find these flowers close to to the ground.

Rodents of Zion

Draw a line from the rodents to its track.

American Beaver

Chipmunk

Rock Squirrel

Porcupine

Big Mammals of Zion

Draw a line from the animal to its track.

Mule Deer

Bighorn Sheep

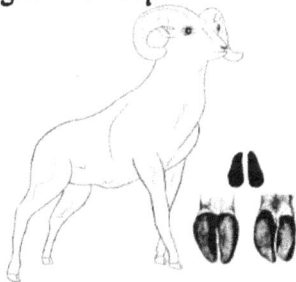

Bobcat

Mountain Lion

Small Mammals of Zion

Draw a line from the animal to its track.

Ringtail

Coyote

Western
Spotted
Skunk

Desert
CottonTail
Rabbit

Match with shadow

Draw a line to match each bird with the correct shadow.

Condor

Hummingbird

Spotted Owl

Quail

Roadrunner

291 bird species can be found in Zion throughout the year.

Match with shadow

Draw a line to match each animal with the correct shadow.

Bighorn Sheep

Bobcat

Grey Fox

Ringtail

Zion is home to 68 species of mammal, ranging from the petite kangaroo rat to the sturdy, surefooted bighorn sheep.

Match with shadow

Draw a line to match each animal with the correct shadow.

Mountain Lion

Coyote

Bat

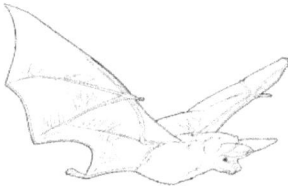

Mule Deer

All throughout Zion, a rich diversity of desert fauna can be seen and experienced.

Match with shadow

Draw a line to match each reptile with the correct shadow.

Greater Short Horned Lizard

Plateau Lizard

Rattlesnake

Desert Tortoise

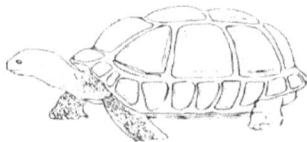

Western Whiptail Lizard

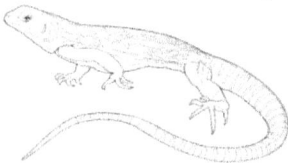

Zion is home to 16 species of lizards, 13 species of snakes and 1 species of tortoise

Match with shadow

Draw a line to match each rodent with the correct shadow.

Beaver

Chipmunk

Porcupine

Rock Squirrel

All rodents have a pair of incisors (teeth) that continue to grow throughout their lives, which they wear down through chewing.

Match with shadow

Draw a line to match each insect with the
correct shadow.

Giant Desert Hairy Scorpion

Desert Tarantula

Globe Mallow Bee

Flame Skimmer Dragonfly

Zion is home to many insects and arachnids.

Match with shadow

Draw a line to match each insect with the correct shadow.

Darkling Beetle

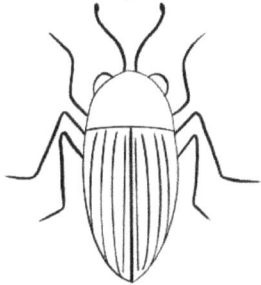

Tarantula Hawk Wasp

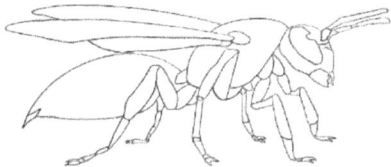

Swallowtail Butterfly

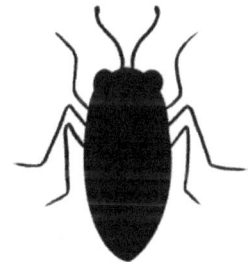

Jerusalem Cricket

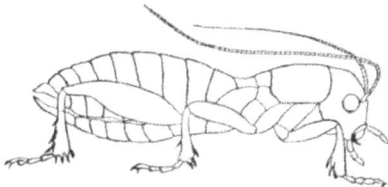

The abundant hiding spaces, food sources, and sunny days allow for a healthy bug population in Zion.

Match with shadow

Draw a line to match each flower with the correct shadow.

Desert
Marigold

Paintbrush

Sacred Datura

Western
Columbine

Zion is home to hundreds of flowering plant species.

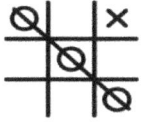

Tic Tac Toe

Challenge your friends and family!

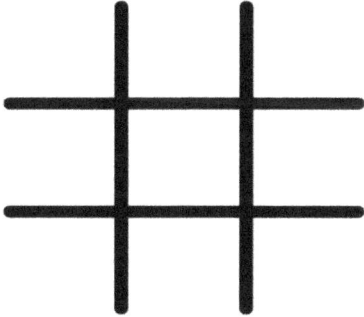
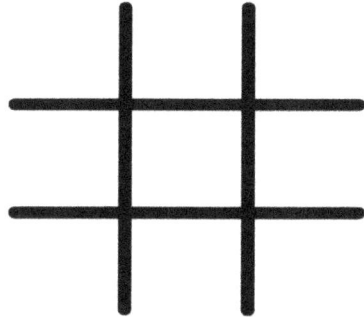

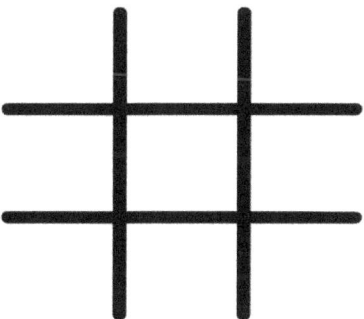
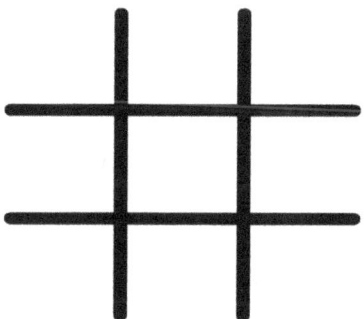

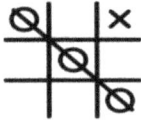

Tic Tac Toe

Challenge your friends and family!

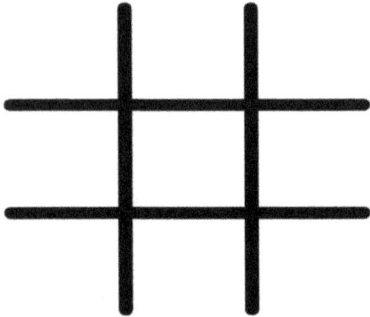

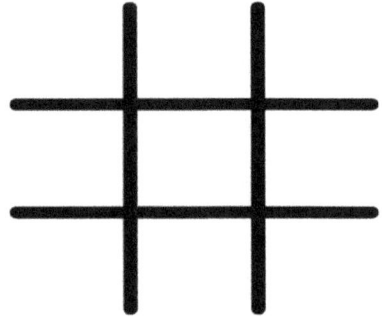

ZION NATIONAL PARK

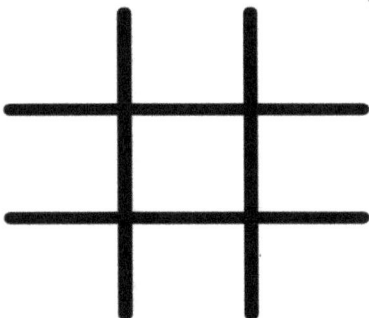

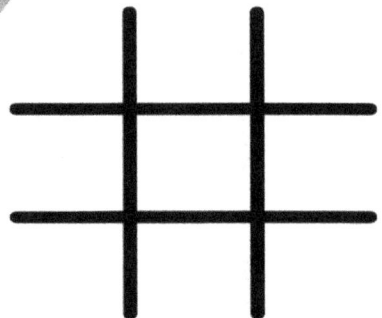

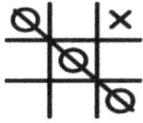

Tic Tac Toe

Challenge your friends and family!

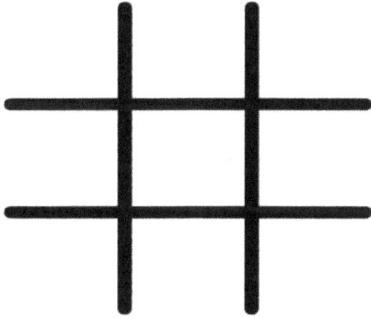

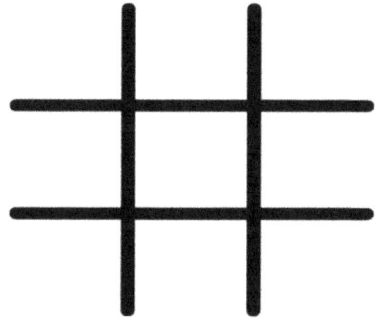

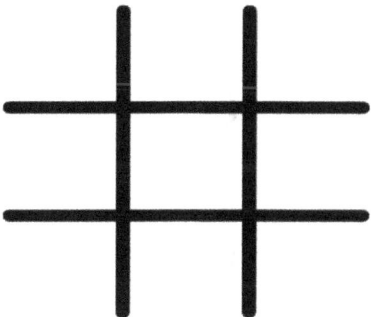

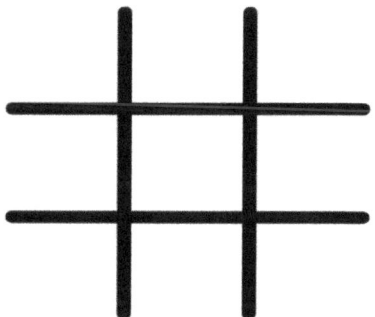

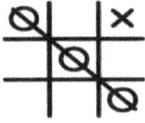

Tic Tac Toe

Challenge your friends and family!

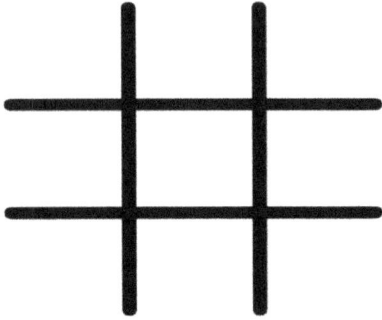

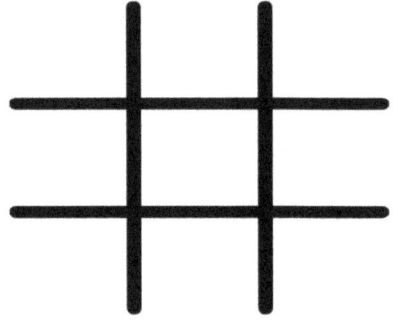

ZION
NATIONAL PARK

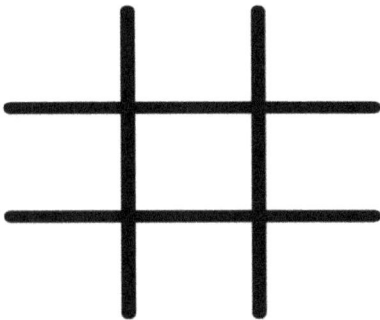

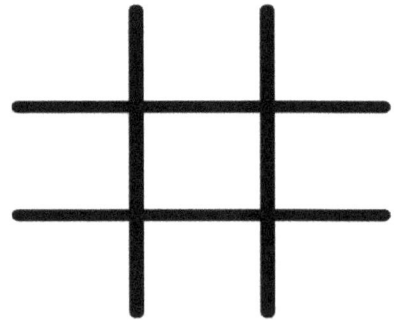

Pattern Completion

Draw or Circle the object that completes the pattern

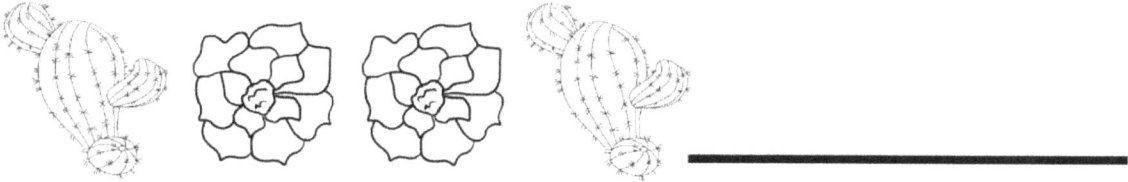

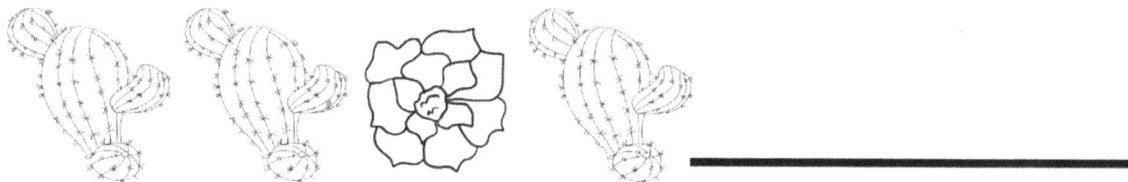

_____

_____

_____

_____

Pattern Completion

Draw or Circle the object that completes the pattern

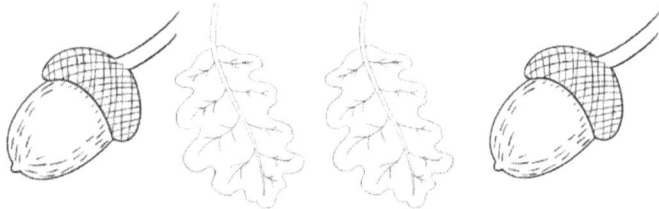

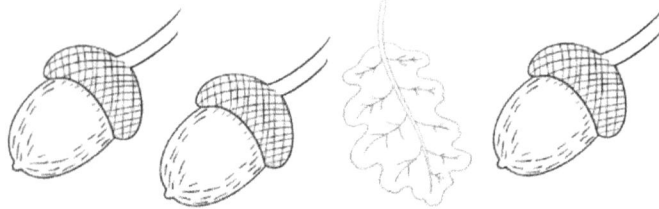

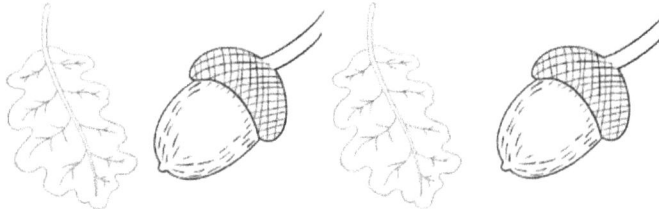

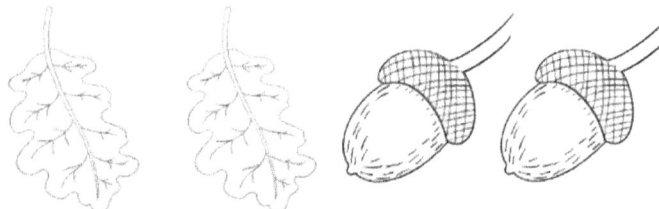

_____

_____

_____

_____

Pattern Completion

Draw or Circle the object that completes the pattern

 _____

 _____

 _____

 _____

Pattern Completion

Draw or Circle the object that completes the pattern

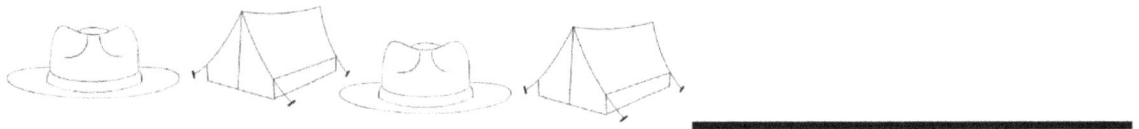 _____

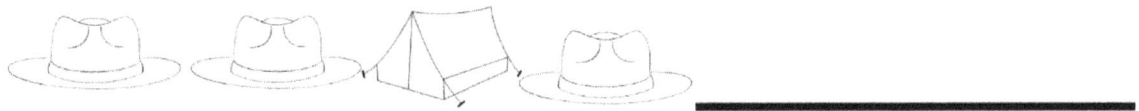 _____

 _____

 _____

Pattern Completion

Draw or Circle the object that completes the pattern

 _____

 _____

 _____

 _____

HOW MANY DRAGONFLIES CAN YOU FIND?

Baby Flame Skimmer Dragonflies are called naiads and they live in the mud at the bottom of the river until they are ready to grow wings and fly   away.

HOW MANY MULE DEER CAN YOU FIND?

Mule deer get their name from their big, mule-like ears.

HOW MANY BIGHORN SHEEP CAN YOU FIND?

Female bighorns are called Ewes
and males are called Rams.

HOW MANY ROADRUNNERS CAN YOU FIND?

Roadrunners run up to 15 miles per hour but can have sprints up to 26 mph.

HOW MANY BOBCATS CAN YOU FIND?

Bobcats get their name from their short tails. Most bobcats have shorter tails than this page!

HOW MANY ROCK SQUIRRELS CAN YOU FIND?

Zion's boulders and cliffs provide an ideal habitat for rock squirrels to build their homes in.

HOW MANY MOUNTAIN LIONS CAN YOU FIND?
Mountain lion cubs have blue eyes and spots.

HOW MANY TARANTULAS CAN YOU FIND?

Tarantulas have a unique defense: they can throw their hair! This hair is irritating and can cause infection, so don't touch them if you see them in the wild.

HOW MANY RINGTAILS CAN YOU FIND?

Ringtails don't need to drink often and can survive for long periods on water derived from food alone.

HOW MANY OWLS CAN YOU FIND?

Spotted Owls are one of the few owls that have dark-colored eyes. Most owls have yellow to red-orange eyes.

Ranger to Ranger Station

Rangers have 2 main responsibilities. Protect the park and the people who visit the park.

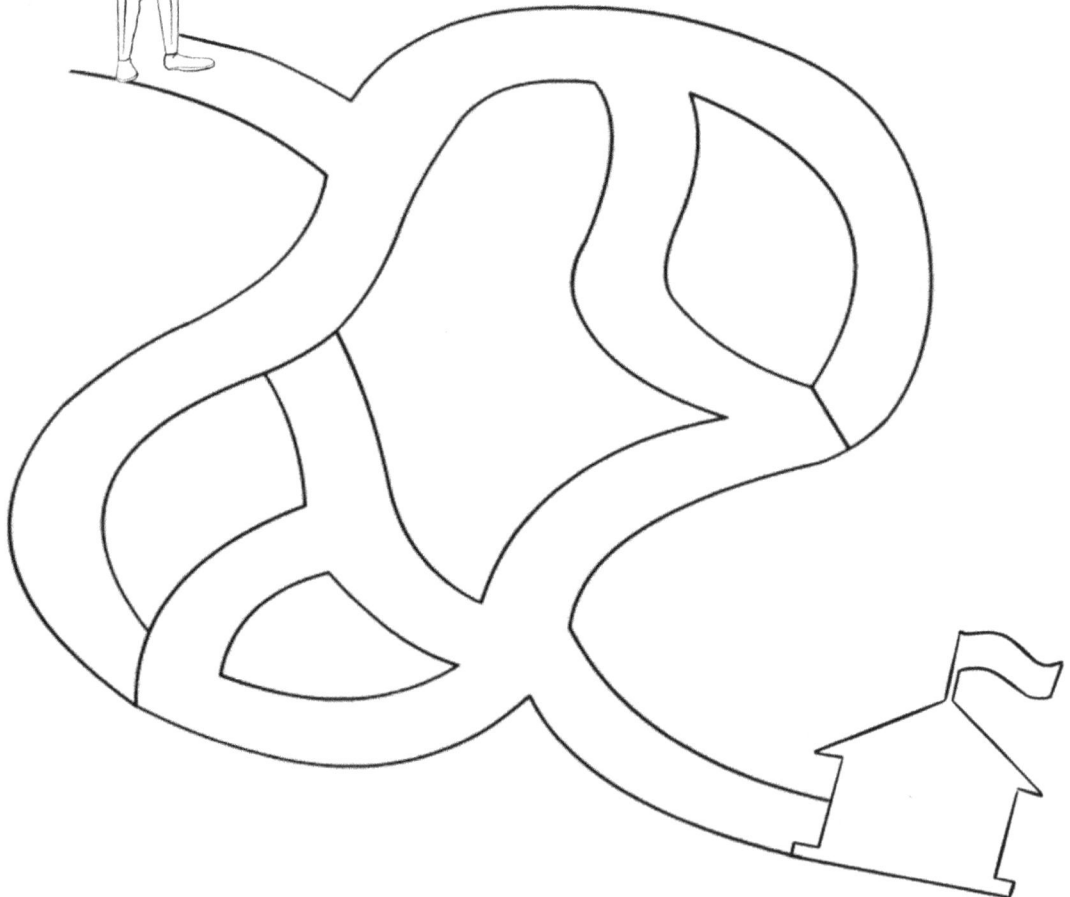

Beaver to Burrow

Baby beavers are called Kits.

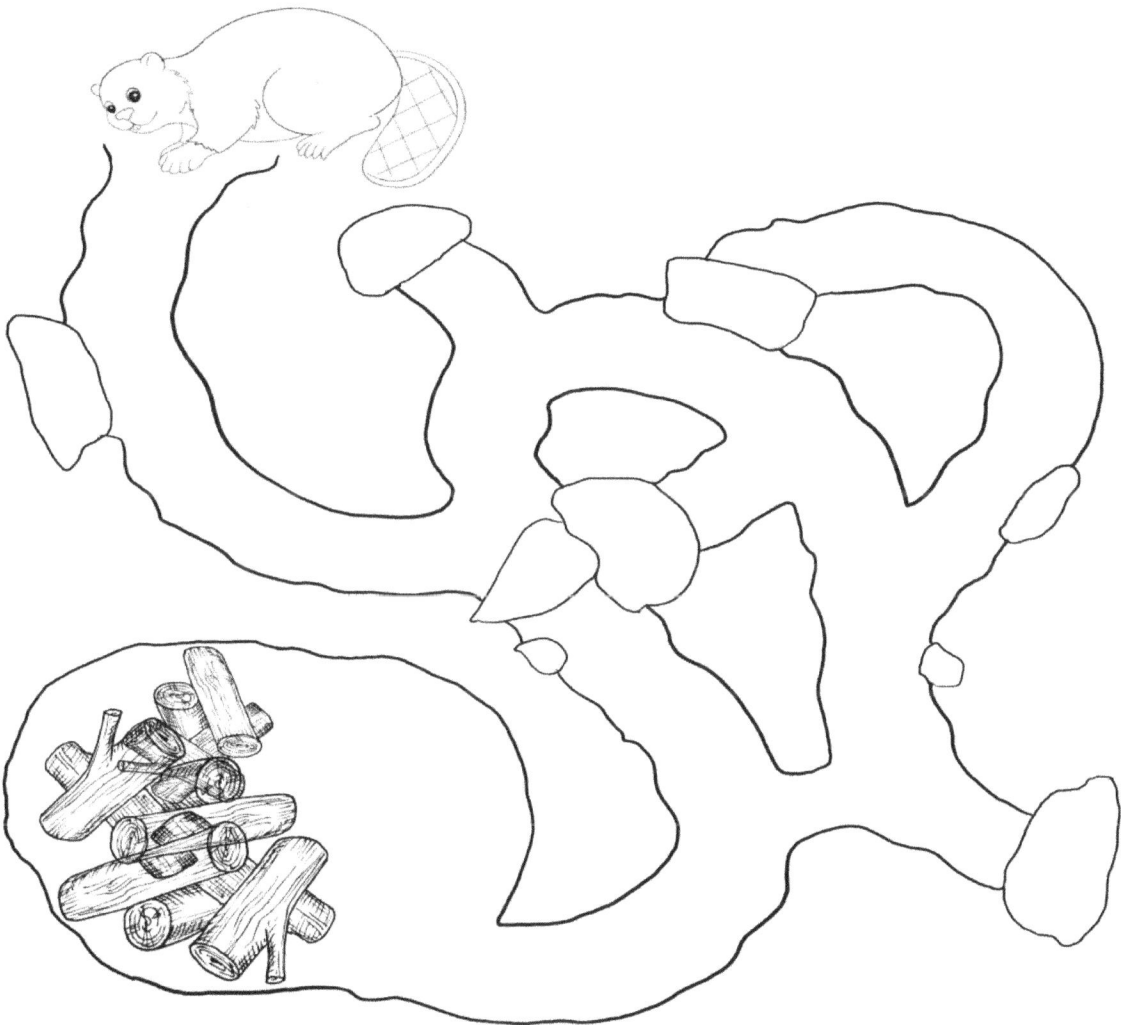

Mountain Lion to River

Mountain Lions can't roar! They communicate by chirping, growling, purring and shrieking.

RoadRunner to Nest

Roadrunners love to sunbathe! They use the sun to warm up in the mornings.

Gray Fox to Den

Gray Foxes are nocturnal, which means they sleep during the day and are active at night.

Bobcat to Den

Bobcats' main food is rodents and rabbits, but have been known to catch fish as well.

Bighorn to top of mountain

The horns on male bighorns can weigh up to 30 lbs!

Hiker through Canyon

Always make sure to bring water and wear good shoes when going for a hike.

Butterfly to Flower Maze

This butterfly's favorite food is
rotting fruit and mud.

Ringtail in Tree-Shaped Maze

Ringtails are often mistaken for part of the cat family since they can climb so high. But they are most closely related to a raccoons

CONNECT THE DOTS

Rough scales on the front legs along with a high domed shell make great defenses for this tortoise

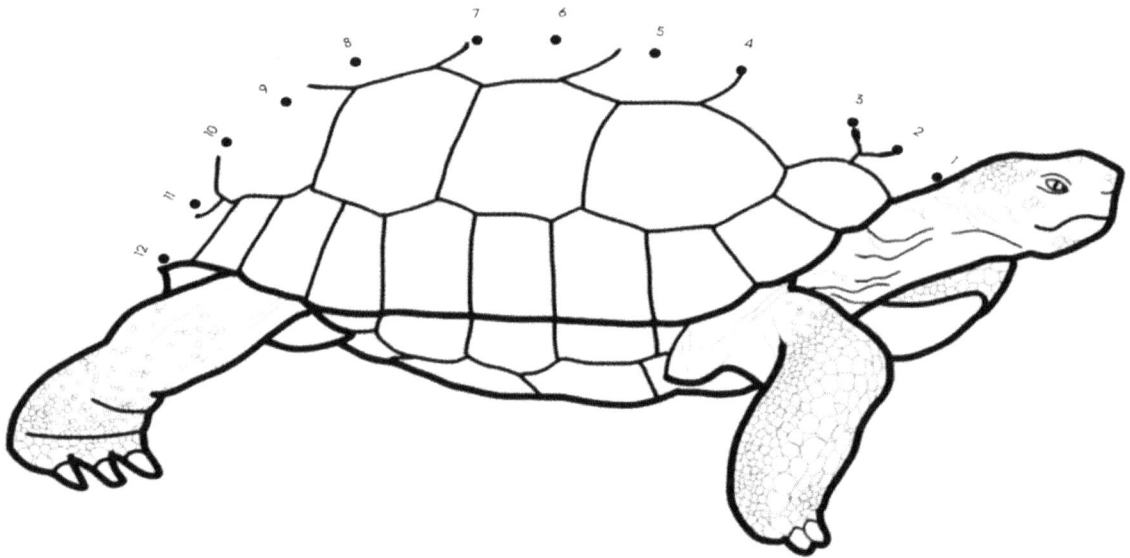

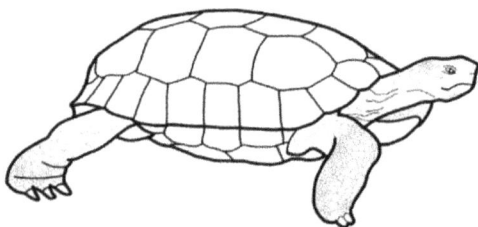

CONNECT THE DOTS

Bobcats can run very fast, up to 30 miles an hour! But not for very far.

CONNECT THE DOTS

Zion's river floods many times a year, beavers who live here, don't build dams, instead they build burrows on the riverbanks

CONNECT THE DOTS

Mexican spotted owls produce 13 different types of barking, hooting, and whistling calls.

CONNECT THE DOTS

This hat protects Park Rangers from the elements but also let's park visitors know that Rangers are 'here to help'

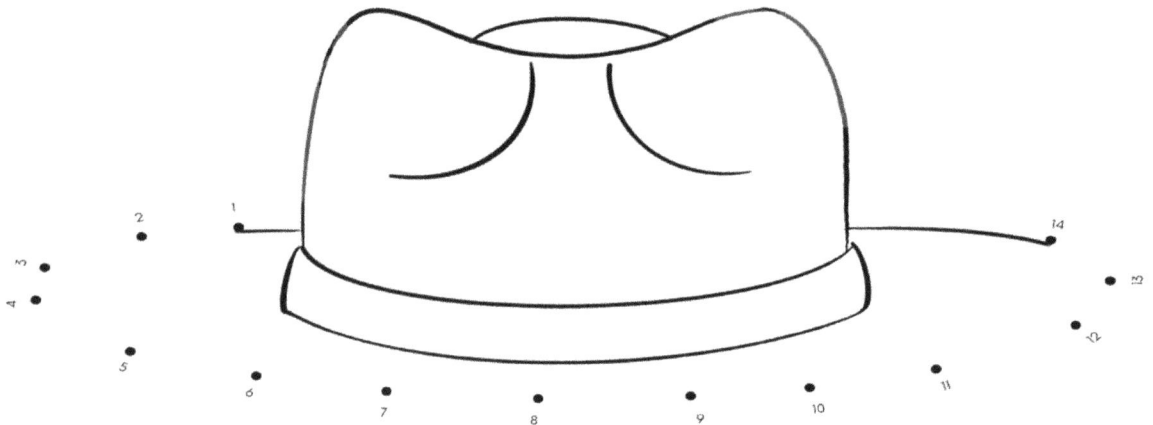

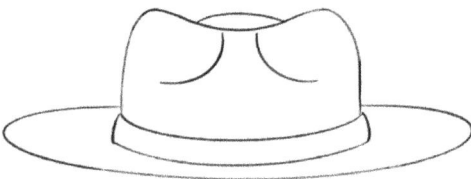

CONNECT THE DOTS

Zion means Sanctuary in Ancient Hebrew

4 •   5 •   6 •   7 •

9 •   10 •   11 •

8 •   12 •   13 •   14 •   15 •

3 •

2 •

1 •

ZION

NATIONAL PARK

ZION
NATIONAL PARK

CONNECT THE DOTS

Bighorn sheep have special hooves that grip the rock and allow them to move up and down the sandstone cliffs.

CONNECT THE DOTS

Roadrunners are graceful on the ground but awkward in the air and typically fly in low, short, bumbling glides onto low branches, or rocks.

1   2   3   4   5

1
2
3
4   5   6

CONNECT THE DOTS

Flame-Skimmers like the heat!
That's why they are found in the
Southwestern part of the U.S.

CONNECT THE DOTS

Mule deer regrow their antlers every year!

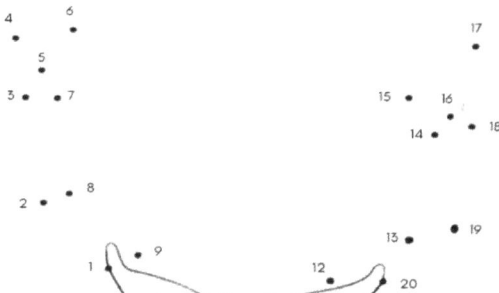

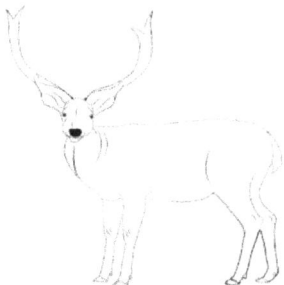

Find the difference

Camping is very popular in Zion National Park

Find the 7 differences in the pictures below

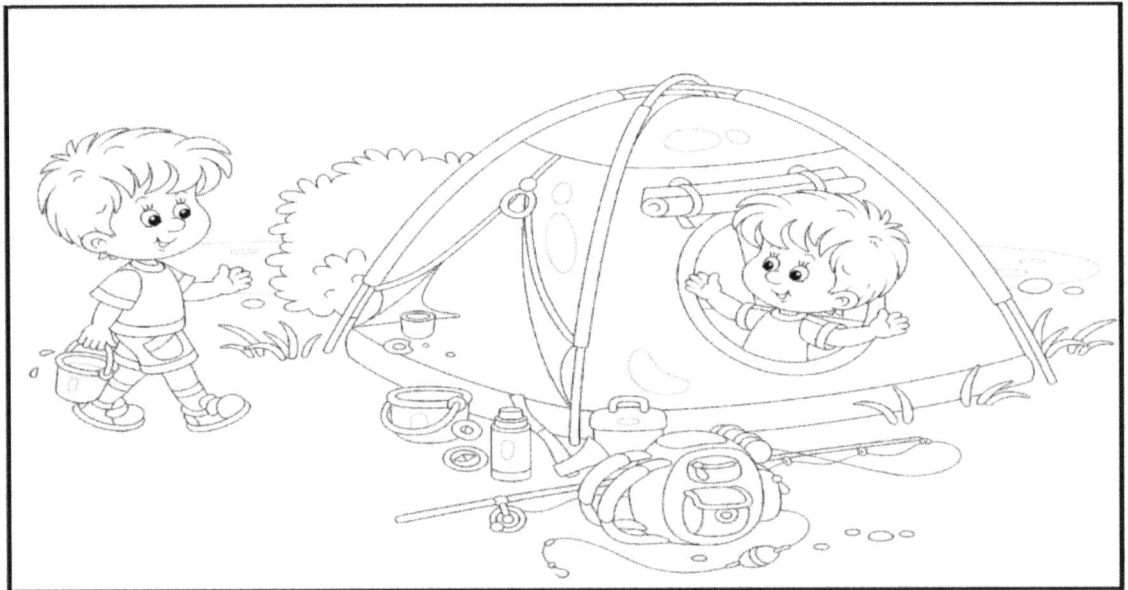

Find the difference

Zion was Utah's First National Park.

Find the 7 differences in the pictures below

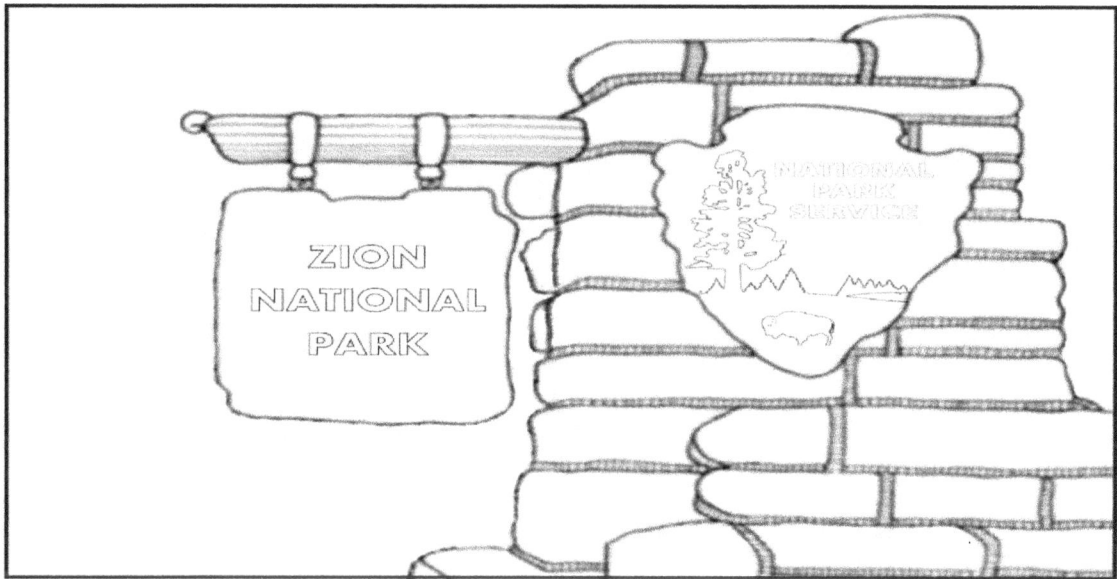

ZION NATIONAL PARK

NATIONAL PARK SERVICE

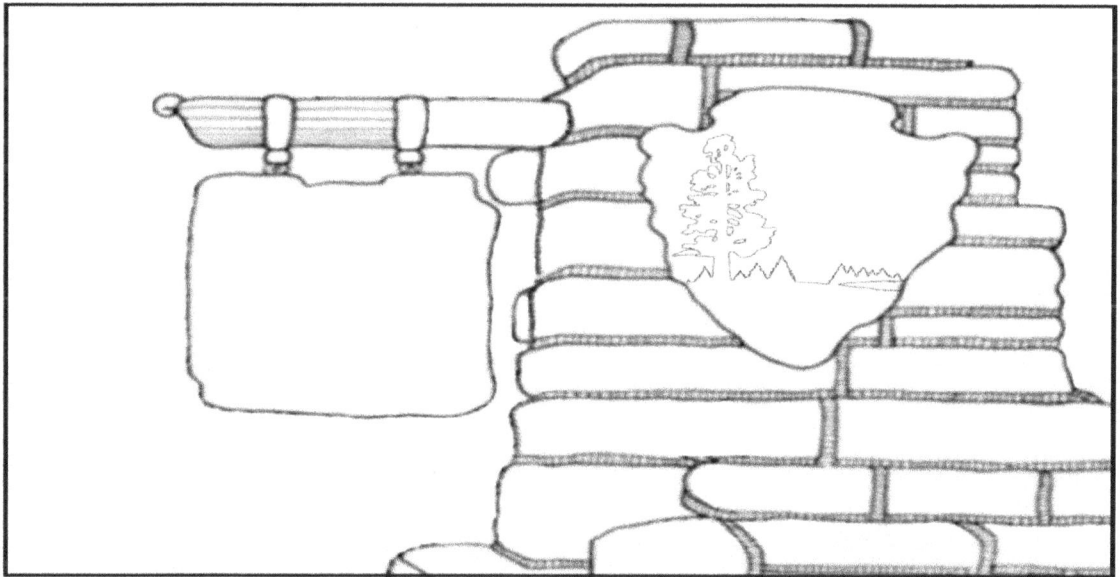

Find the difference

Dragonflies spend most of their lives living as naiads under the water.

Find the 7 differences in the pictures below

Find the difference

Bobcats can have up to 6 babies in a litter.

Find the 7 differences in the pictures below

Find the difference

Zion's hanging gardens are the most popular plant life in the park.

Find the 7 differences in the pictures below

Find the difference

Baby deer are called fawns and are born with white spots on their fur.

Find the 7 differences in the pictures below

Find the difference

Cottontail rabbits' teeth never stop growing. The tough grasses they eat help to wear the teeth down continually to make sure that they don't get too long.

Find the 7 differences in the pictures below

Find the difference

Ringtails are nocturnal, which means they are mostly active during the night and inactive during the day.

Find the 7 differences in the pictures below

Find the difference

Hiking is a great way to get exercise and to see nature up close.

Find the 7 differences in the pictures below

Find the difference

Tarantulas climb with the aid of retractable claws that are at the end of each leg.

Find the 7 differences in the pictures below

Draw the rings on the Ringtail

Ringtails are omnivores, which means they eat both plants and animals

Draw eyes on the Owl

Owls in Zion typically eat desert woodrats
and occasionally darkling beetles

Draw the spikes on the Porcupine

Porcupines are more common in higher elevation forests, but they can also be found in lower elevation riparian zones and even deserts—all habitats found within Zion.

Draw the hat on the Park Ranger

Rangers love answering questions from visitors.
What would you like to ask a Ranger?

Draw the ears on the Bobcat

Bobcat's footprints don't include their claws like coyotes. This is because their claws are retractable, meaning they go back into their paws when not needed.

Draw the hanging garden on the cliff wall

With elevations ranging from roughly 3,700 to 8,700 feet, Zion National Park has a diversity of plant communities, supporting more than 1,000 species of plants

Draw the horns on the BigHorn Sheep

If you are looking for BigHorns in Zion, look up!

They climb cliff walls to stay clear of predators.

Draw the horns on the Mule Deer

Mule Deer are very common in Zion. Though they may get close, it's important not to touch or feed them.

Draw the hiker on the trail

When hiking remember the motto: Take only photographs and leave only footprints.

Make your own Park Badge

GREAT BASIN RATTLESNAKE

THE GREAT BASIN RATTLESNAKE IS ZION'S ONLY VENOMOUS SNAKE

LEAVE NO TRACE

IT IS IMPORTANT TO PRESERVE THE NATURAL BEAUTY OF NATURE BY BEING MINDFUL OF HOW WE INTERACT WITH IT.

GREATER SHORT-HORNED LIZARD

THIS LIZARD DEFENDS ITSELF WITH IT'S HORNS AND THE ABILITY TO SHOOT BLOOD FROM IT'S TEAR DUCTS

THE NARROWS

TO HIKE IN THE NARROWS PREPARE TO GET WET!

ZION
NATIONAL PARK

DESERT
TARANTULA

TARANTULAS ARE THE LARGEST SPIDERS IN THE SOUTHWEST

AMERICAN BEAVER

LARGE FLAT TAILS AND WEBBED BACK FEET HELP
BEAVERS SWIM

HUMMINGBIRD

THE BEST PLACE TO SEE HUMMINGBIRDS IN ZION IS CLOSE TO THE VIRGIN RIVER

ROCK SQUIRREL

WHILE THEY MAY APPROACH YOU AND LOOK ADORABLE, IT IS
IMPORTANT TO NOT FEED THE SQUIRRELS, OR ANY OTHER WILDLIFE.

· Z I O N ·

NATIONAL PARK

U T A H

PAINTBRUSH FLOWER

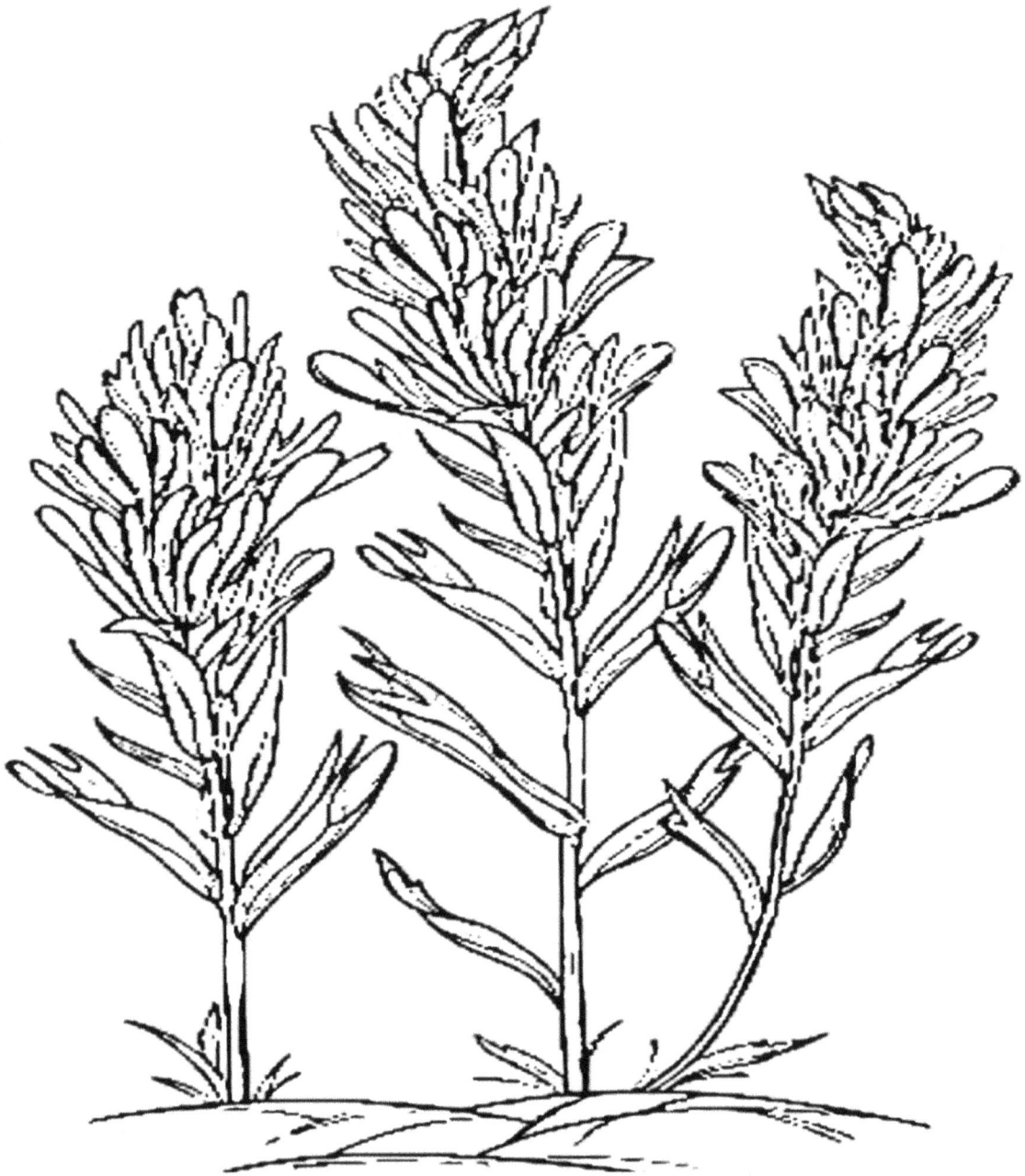

CAN YOU GUESS HOW THIS FLOWER GOT IT'S NAME?

GLOBEMALLOW FLOWERS

THIS DELICATE ORANGE FLOWERS CAN BE FOUND ALL OVER THE PARK

PARK RANGER

RANGERS ARE A WEALTH OF INFORMATION ABOUT THE ANIMALS AND NATURAL FEATURES OF A PARK.

BUTTERFLY

BUMBLEBEE AND
PINK THISTLE FLOWER

DESERT

TORTOUISE

DESERT TORTOUISES LIVE ALMOST ALL THEIR LIVES IN UNDERGROUND BURROWS, AVOIDING THE HEAT OF SUMMER IN A SEMI-DORMANT STATE AND HIBERNATING IN WINTER.

CAMPING

MULE DEER LIKE TO VISIT THE CAMPGROUNDS IN ZION, SO BE
SURE NOT TO LEAVE ANY FOOD OUT UNATTENDED

TIGER
SALAMANDER

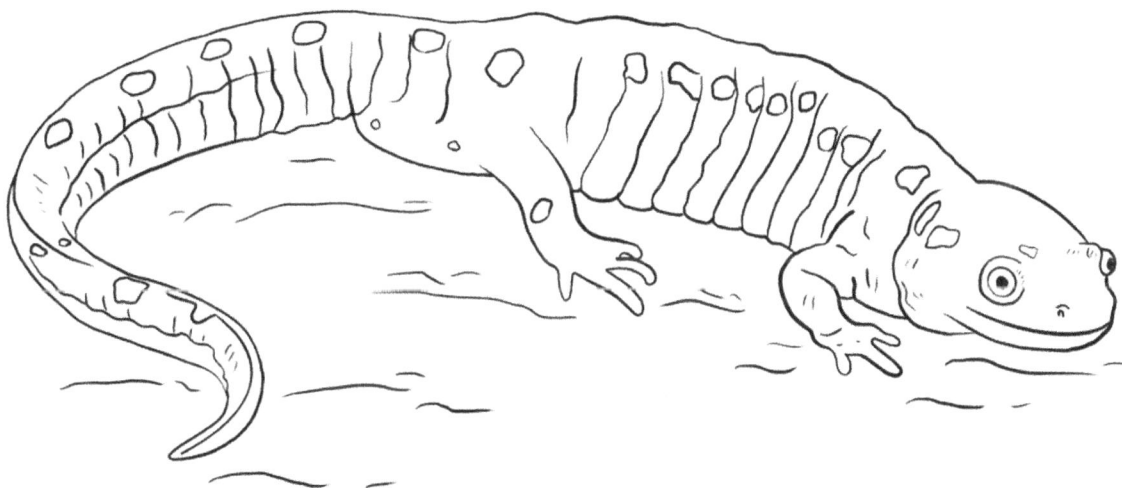

THIS IS THE WORLD'S LARGEST LAND-DWELLING SALAMANDER.

CANYON
TREE FROG

A VERY DISTINCTIVE FEATURE OF THIS FROG IS SUCTION DISCS ON EACH TOE.

GIANT DESERT HAIRY SCORPION

THIS SCORPION GETS IT'S NAME FROM WHERE IT LIVES AND THE SMALL HAIRS ON IT'S LEGS.

DESERT BIGHORN SHEEP

DESERT BIGHORNS HAVE SMALLER BODIES BUT LONGER LEGS THAN
THEIR COUSINS, THE ROCKY MOUNTAIN BIGHORN.

BANANA YUCCA FLOWER

YUCCA FLOWERS ONLY HAVE ONE POLLINATOR, THE YUCCA MOTH.

GAMBEL'S QUAIL

THE QUAIL'S LONG-TOED FEET ALLOW FOR WALKING AND FEEDING ON THE GROUND IN SEARCH OF SEEDS, INSECTS, AND WATER.

FOURWING SALTBUSH

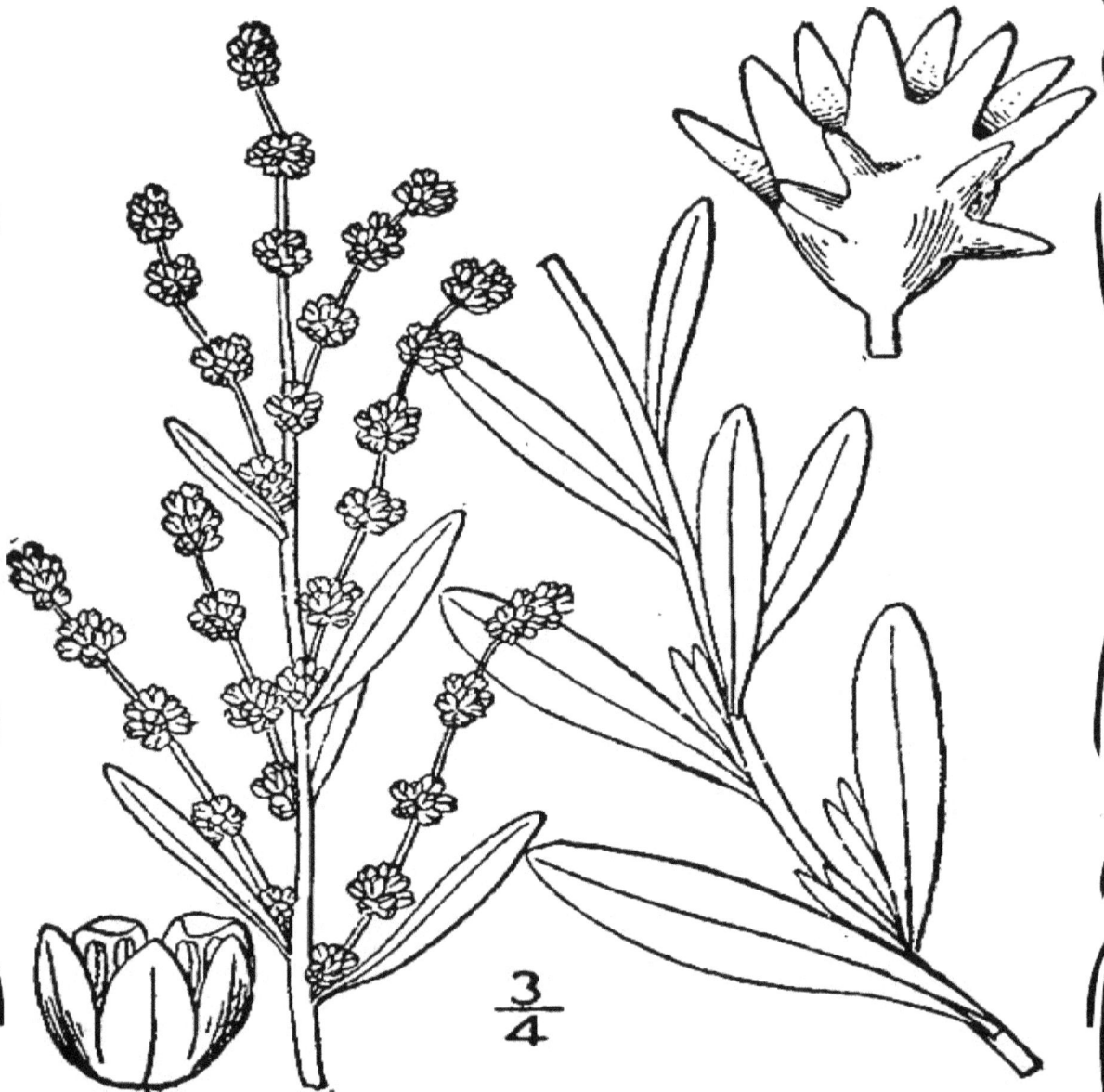

$\frac{3}{4}$

THESE FASCINATING SHRUBS CAN RID THEMSELVES OF EXCESS SALT THROUGH THE TINY HAIRS ON THE LEAVES. THE HAIRS THEN DIE, LEAVING DEPOSITS OF SALT CRYSTALS THAT REFLECT THE INTENSE DESERT SUNLIGHT.

GREATER ROADRUNNER

THESE TOUGH BIRDS CAN CATCH AND EAT SNAKES!

www.ingramcontent.com/pod-product-compliance
Lightning Source LLC
Chambersburg PA
CBHW080423030426
42335CB00020B/2559